potholder
loom designs

140 Colorful Patterns

SCHIFFER
PUBLISHING

4880 Lower Valley Road • Atglen, PA 19310

Table of Contents

Introduction

Weaving is a centuries-old technique that has long been thought of in terms of its utilitarian purposes. Today, it's also appreciated as a creative outlet that is used for crafting, hobby, and fine art. Potholder weaving is a craft that brings together the functional and artistic components of weaving and uses the loom as a tool to create effortless designs with an almost instant result.

At Harrisville Designs we see potholder weaving as a fun but exciting activity that helps people create something tangible and tactile, and that can be done with a few high-quality materials in everyday spaces. Our Potholder Looms & Loops are thoughtfully made in the USA, and we have chosen materials that will stand the test of time. All the weaving patterns in this book are made on our sturdy metal looms, with real cotton loops.

Potholder weaving is a nostalgic technique and for some people brings back fond memories from their childhood. We believe it is a craft for all ages and skill levels, often bringing people together in creative gathering. In part, this is why we love what we do at Harrisville Designs, and we are so grateful to help foster the growth of our weaving community. We hope you'll enjoy weaving the designs featured in this book and forever become part of our weaving story.

About Harrisville Designs

Woolen yarn has been spun in Harrisville, New Hampshire, for over 200 years. Harrisville Designs is a small, family-operated business that began in 1971 and is carrying on that textile tradition. We make high-quality, natural 100% wool yarns for knitting and weaving along with beautiful carded fleece for felting and spinning. We also produce floor looms in several styles, weaving tools and accessories, and our wonderful line of award-winning fiber craft products, including potholder looms and loops.

Parts of the Loom
& Supplies You'll Need

All the supplies needed for weaving a potholder are included in the Traditional Size Potholder Loom Kit. Please note that the sides of the loom are labeled A, B, C, and D—you will need to reference these to follow along with the instructions on the following pages.

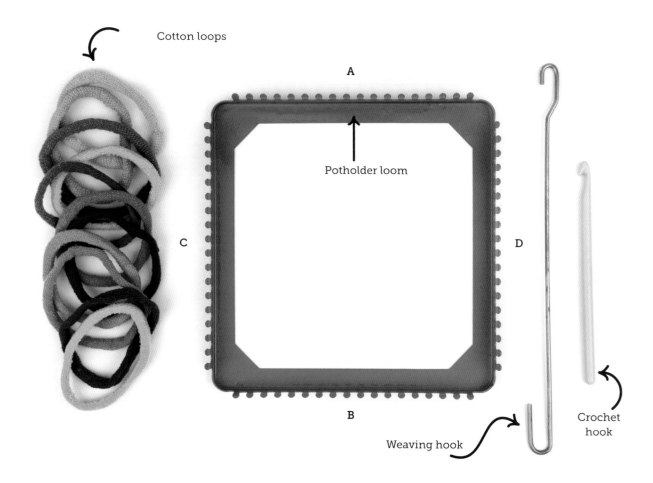

Cotton loops

A

Potholder loom

C

D

B

Weaving hook

Crochet hook

How to Weave a Potholder

1   Warping Your Loom

Using the colors you like best, stretch loops over the pegs from the top (A) to the bottom (B), as shown, covering all of them.

2   Weaving

Row 1: Start on side D, holding the large end of the weaving hook. Go under and over every other loop (2 strands) until the small hook comes out at side C. Pull a loop, using the small end of the hook, from side C through to side D. Attach the ends of the loops to the bottom pegs both on sides C and D. Push the loop down toward the bottom of the loom to make it straight.

Row 2: Using your weaving hook (and starting on side D), pass it over and under the opposite loops from the last time. So, if you went under the first loop (2 strands), now go over them and under the second loop (2 strands). Repeat this all the way across. Attach ends of loops as before and push the loop down against the first loop. Repeat this sequence until you have covered all the pegs on sides C and D.

3   Finishing the Edges & Taking the Potholder off the Loom

Using the plastic crochet hook, pull off the first loop at the top right-side corner. Keeping the first loop on the hook, move to the left and put the hook through the second loop, pulling off and through the first loop. You will have one loop left on your hook.

Again, moving to the left, put the hook through the third loop and pull it through the second. Continue this around the entire potholder until you come to the last loop. *Important: See tip below before finishing off all sides.* Take the last loop off the hook and pull it tight. This is the loop you will hang your potholder with.

Finishing Tip

After you finish one side of the potholder, hook a middle loop onto one of the metal pegs of the loom. That way the potholder will stay in place and out of your way as you continue finishing the other sides. Or you can use some paper clips or big safety pins to hold the loops in place. Some people put a heavy elastic band over all of the loops on each unfinished side to keep them from popping off!

Color Guide

We make custom-sized cotton loops in 34 colors that are made to fit both the Traditional Size Loom (7" × 7") and the PRO Size Loom (10" × 10"). Our loops come in three color lines: Bright, Pastel, and Designer.

Bright Line

Plum	Purple	Pink	Salmon	Red	Orange	Yellow	Green

Lime	Peacock	Turquoise	Blue	White	Black

Pastel Line

Robin's Egg	Powder Blue	Hydrangea	Lavender	Carnation	Tiger Lily	Daffodil	Leaf

Designer Line

Dark Navy	Burgundy	Pine	Willow	Flax	Ochre	Spice	Autumn

Chocolate	Winter White	Silver	Pewter

Traditional-Size Potholder Designs

In this section you'll find designs for our Traditional Potholder Loom, which is custom made of sturdy metal—just the way you remember it to be. The Traditional Potholder Loom measures 7" × 7" and makes 6" × 6" potholders.

All of our looms, loops, and potholder kits are made with top-quality materials, manufactured in the USA. Not only will they stand the test of time, but weaving on one of our Potholder Looms is meditative and relaxing. For children, potholder weaving is a fun, educational experience that helps develop concentration, fine and gross motor control, and a better understanding of spatial relationships and patterning. Potholder weaving is a creative outlet spanning all ages that builds a tactile experience in creating something beautiful and practical to own, or to give.

Color & Design

There are many ways to change the colors and make new patterns on your Potholder Loom. We hope you will explore weaving the patterns designed in this book, and become inspired to create your own projects. We've built a helpful design tool called the Potholder Pattern Wizard, which will generate weaving patterns by using your favorite loop colors from all three color lines. You can explore this tool online, at www.harrisville.com. If you prefer an analog approach, you can also create weaving patterns using graph paper and colored pencils.

The potholder patterns in this book are formatted to mirror the way our Potholder Pattern Wizard generates designs. To read the pattern, follow the color bubbles sur-rounding the design and stretch the loops onto your loom in the color order you see. Please note that if you like a pattern but you do not like the color combination chosen, you may interchange one or more of the colors represented in the design with new colors. Happy weaving!

Bright Color Line

Find the weaving pattern for this potholder on page 17.

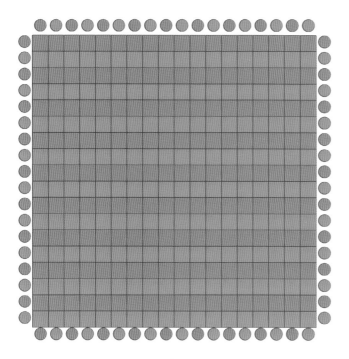

Pink, Salmon

Lime, Peacock, Yellow, Orange, Red, Salmon, Pink,
Purple, Plum, White

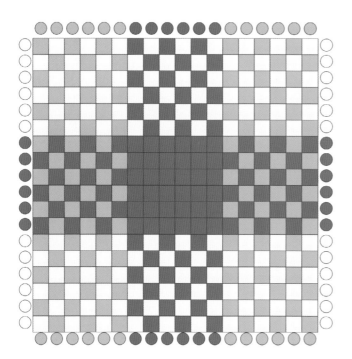

Lime, Peacock, White

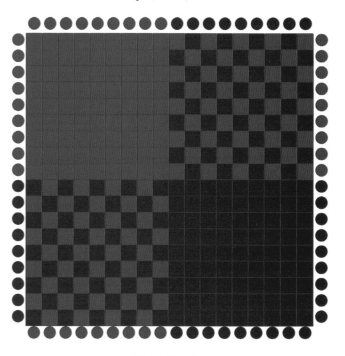

Plum, Purple

Find the weaving pattern for this potholder on page 14.

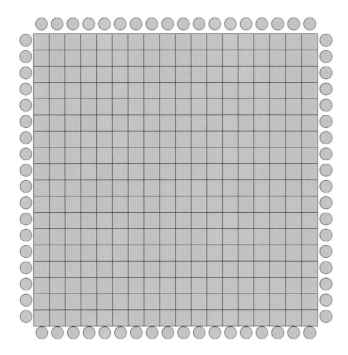

Yellow, Lime

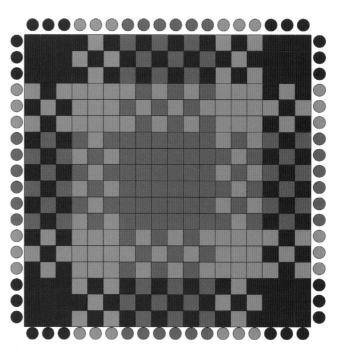

Turquoise, Peacock, Blue

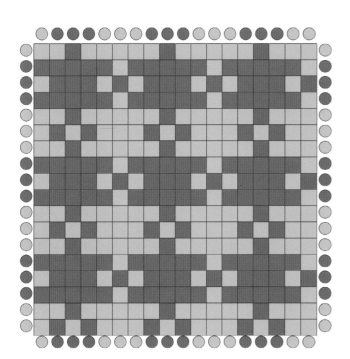

Lime, Turquoise

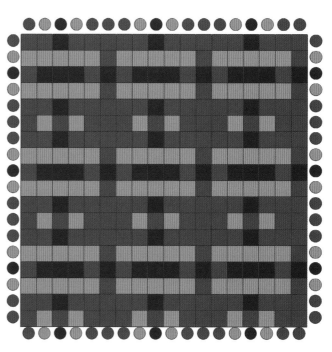

Plum, Purple, Pink

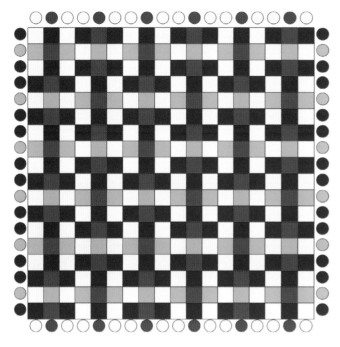

Lime, Purple, Plum, White

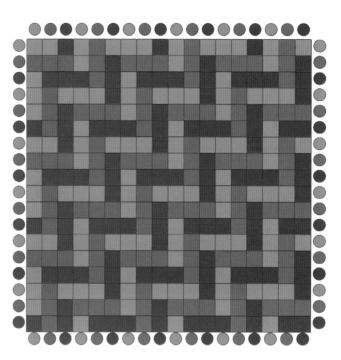

Plum, Peacock, Turquoise

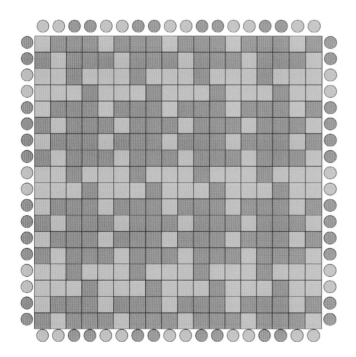

Salmon, Yellow

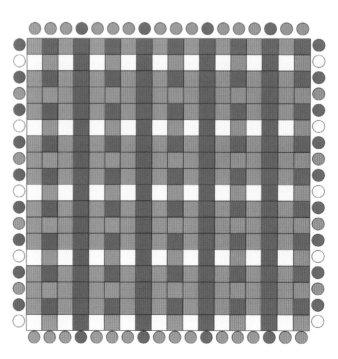

Salmon, Peacock, White

Pastel Color Line

Find the weaving pattern for this potholder on page 19.

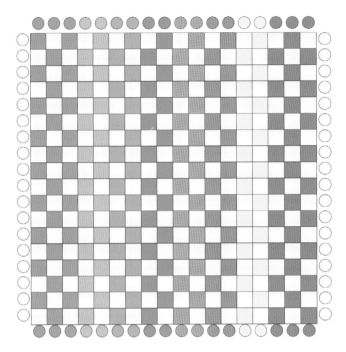

Robin's Egg, Powder Blue, Hydrangea, Lavender,
Carnation, Tiger Lily, Daffodil, Leaf, White

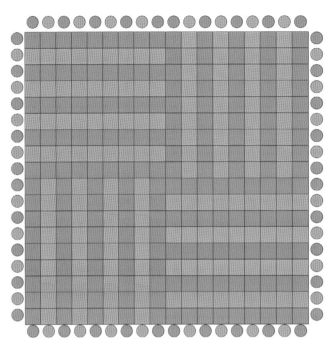

Carnation, Tiger Lily

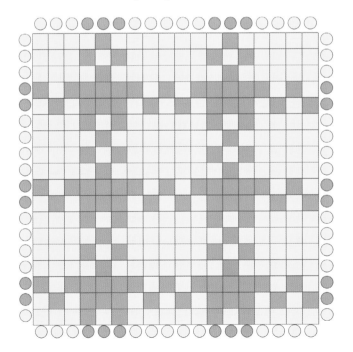

Hydrangea, Daffodil

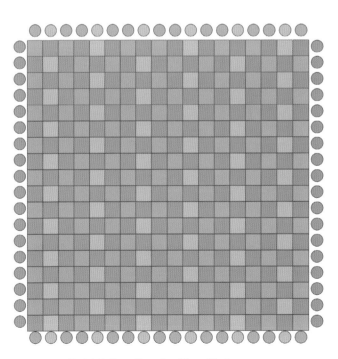

Robin's Egg, Powder Blue, Hydrangea

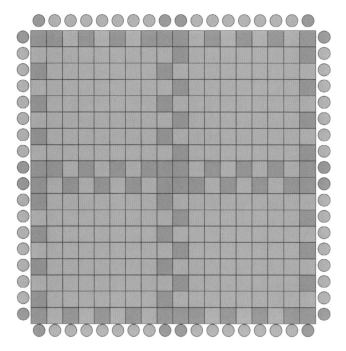

Hydrangea, Lavender

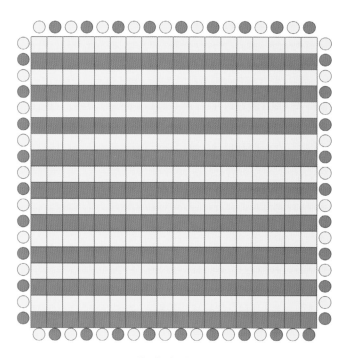

Daffodil, Leaf

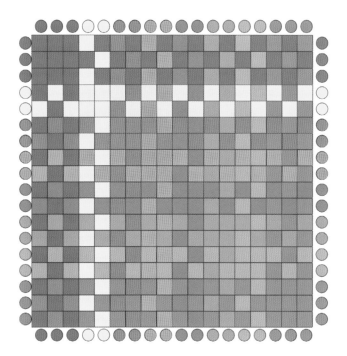

Robin's Egg, Powder Blue, Hydrangea, Lavender,
Carnation, Tiger Lily, Daffodil, Leaf

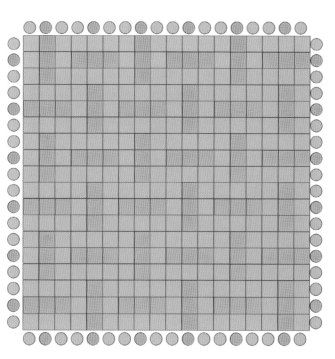

Powder Blue, Carnation

Find the weaving pattern for this potholder on page 20.

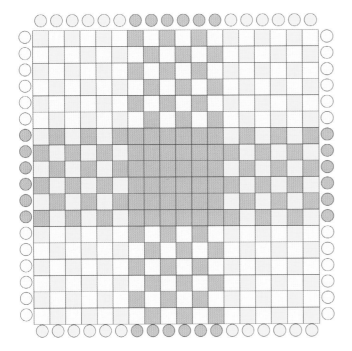

Powder Blue, Daffodil, White

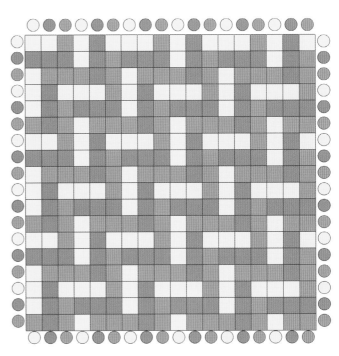

Carnation, Tiger Lily, Daffodil

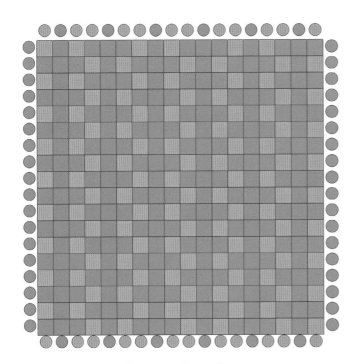

Lavender, Carnation

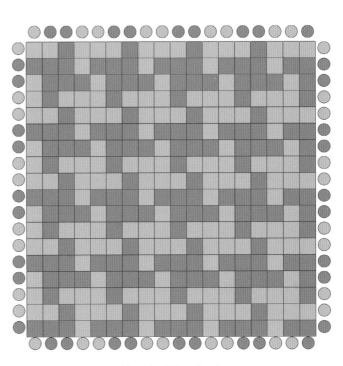

Powder Blue, Leaf

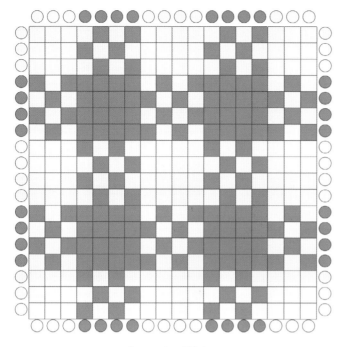

Lavender, White

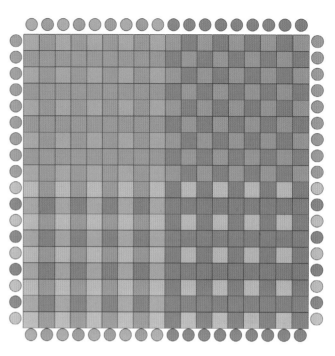

Robin's Egg, Powder Blue, Hydrangea, Leaf

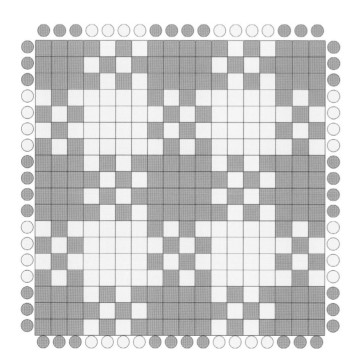

Carnation, Daffodil

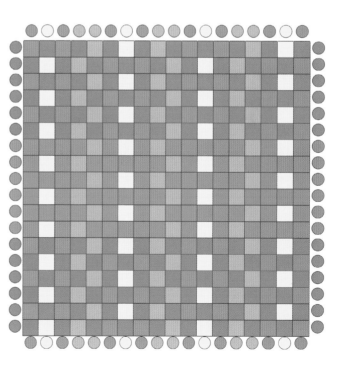

Robin's Egg, Powder Blue, Lavender, Daffodil

Designer Color Line

Find the weaving pattern for this potholder on page 25.

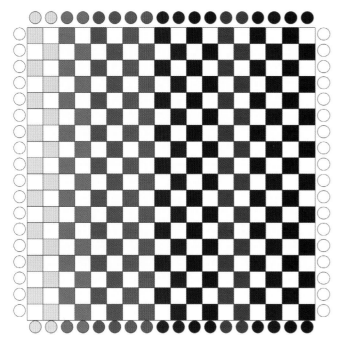

Flax, Autumn, Ochre, Spice, Burgundy, Pine, Willow,
Dark Navy, Winter White

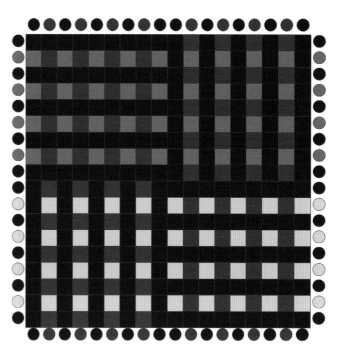

Pine, Willow, Flax, Autumn

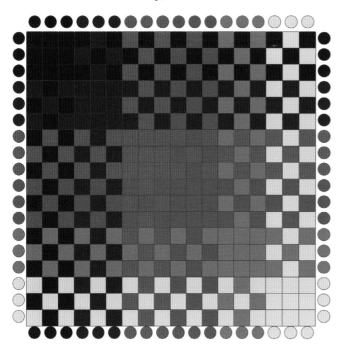

Chocolate, Burgundy, Spice, Ochre, Autumn, Flax

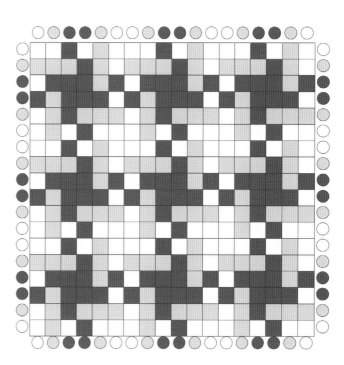

Flax, Spice, Winter White

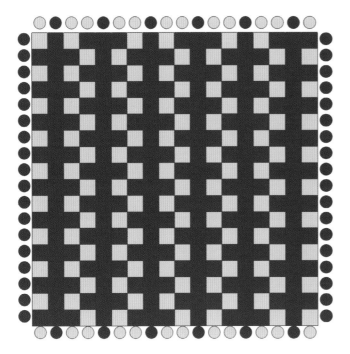

Flax, Willow

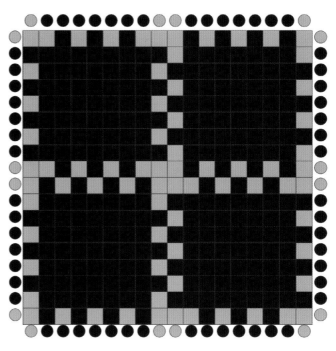

Dark Navy, Silver

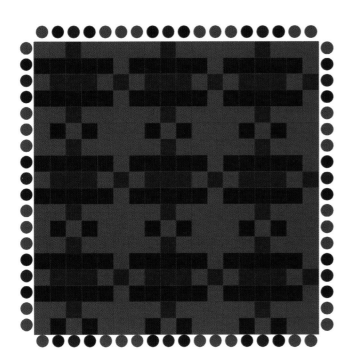

Willow, Chocolate, Burgundy

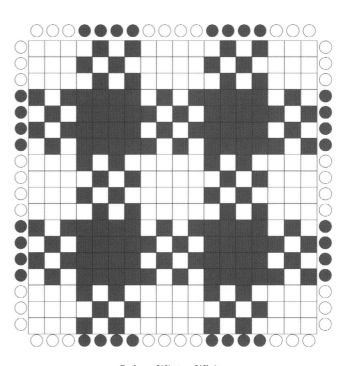

Ochre, Winter White

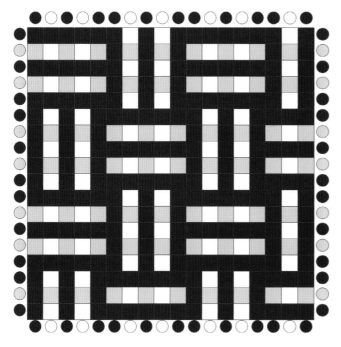

Burgundy, Flax, Winter White

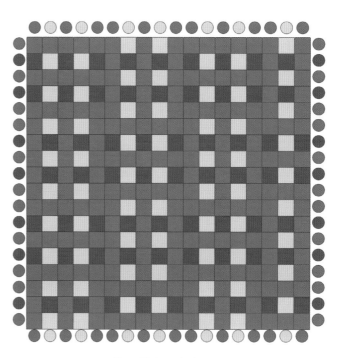

Flax, Ochre, Autumn

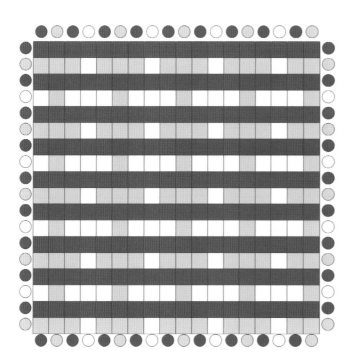

Flax, Ochre, Spice, Winter White

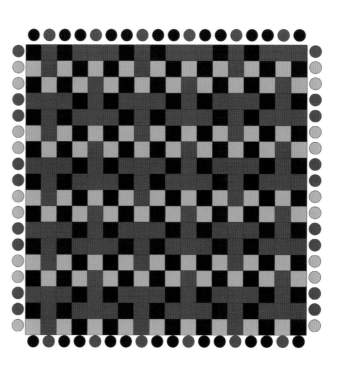

Dark Navy, Silver, Pewter

Find the weaving pattern for this potholder on page 29.

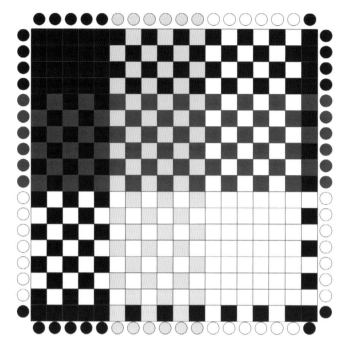

Pine, Willow, Flax, Winter White

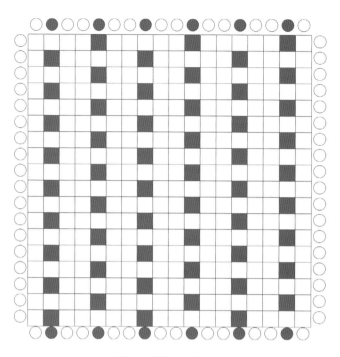

Winter White, Spice

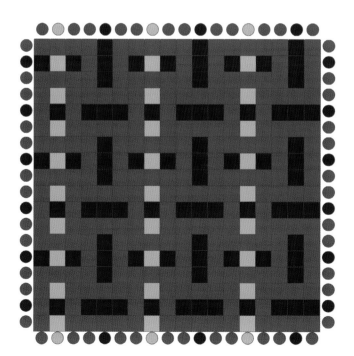

Pewter, Silver, Chocolate

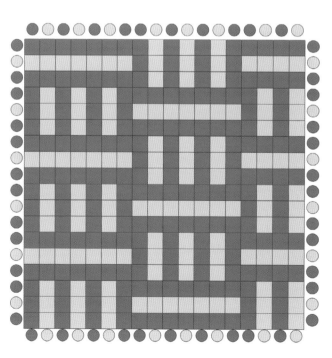

Ochre, Flax

Black & White

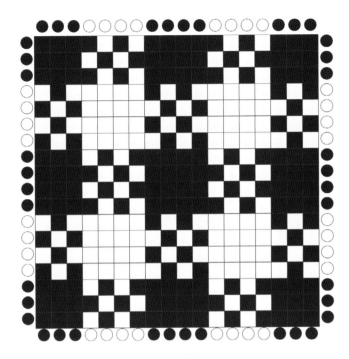

Black, White

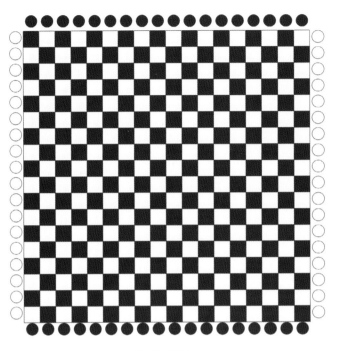

Black, White

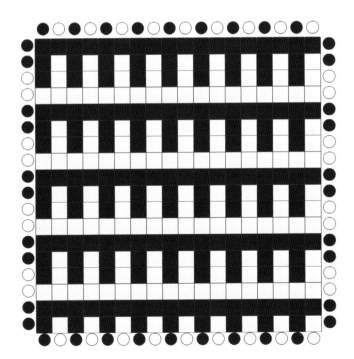

Black, White

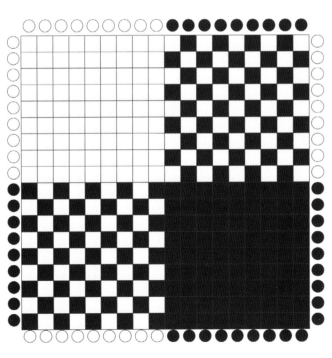

Black, White

One-Color

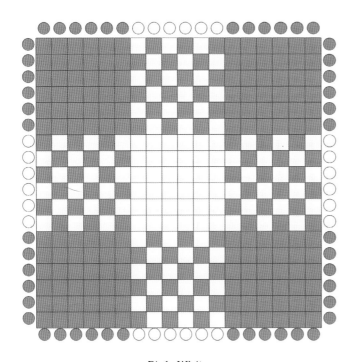

Pink, White

Turquoise, White

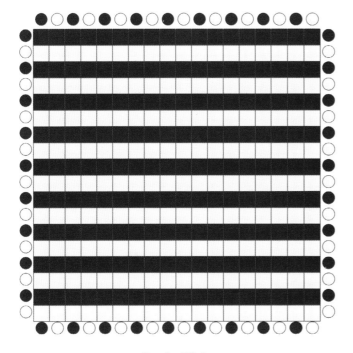

Purple, White

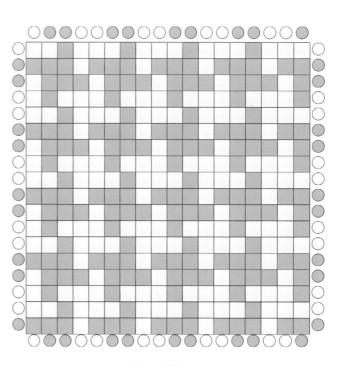

Lime, White

Plaid

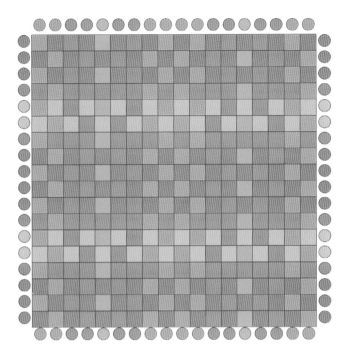

Carnation, Pink, Salmon, Hydrangea, Powder Blue

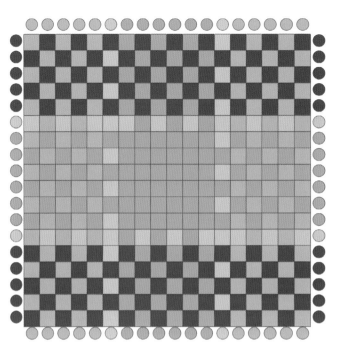

Hydrangea, Powder Blue, Robin's Egg, Plum

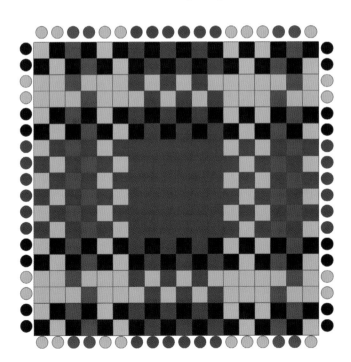

Silver, Pewter, Dark Navy, Willow

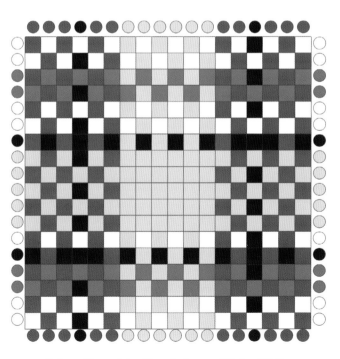

Ochre, Chocolate, Flax, Autumn, Winter White

Find the weaving pattern for this potholder on page 32.

Tonal

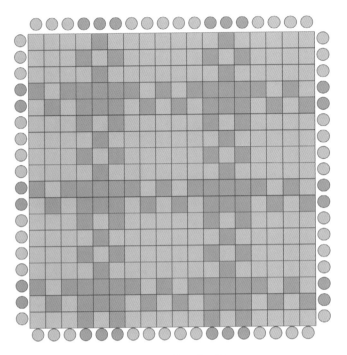

Robin's Egg, Powder Blue

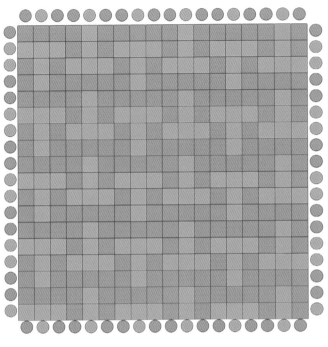

Carnation, Salmon

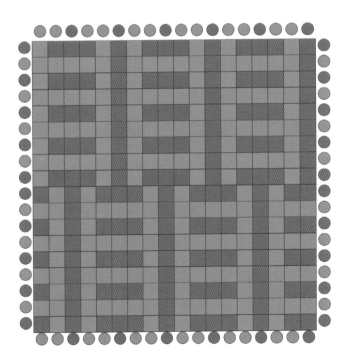

Orange, Tiger Lily

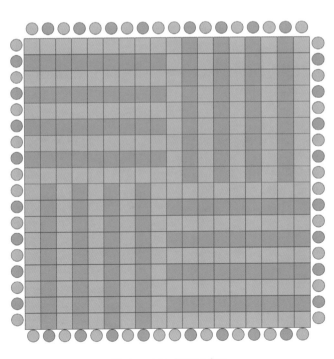

Hydrangea, Lavender

Color Pops

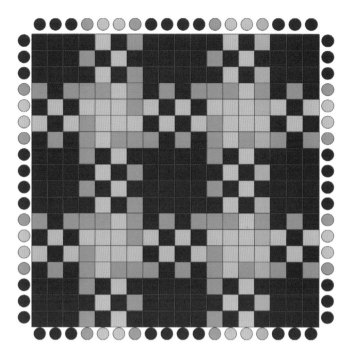

Purple, Hydrangea, Powder Blue

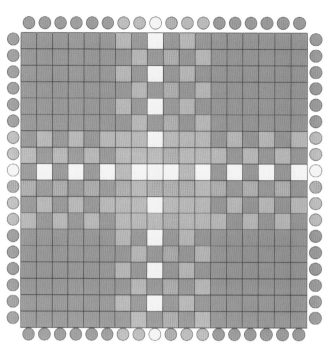

Robin's Egg, Powder Blue, Carnation, Daffodil

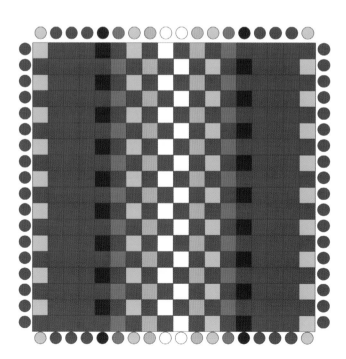

Lime, Pewter, Black, Peacock, Silver, Winter White

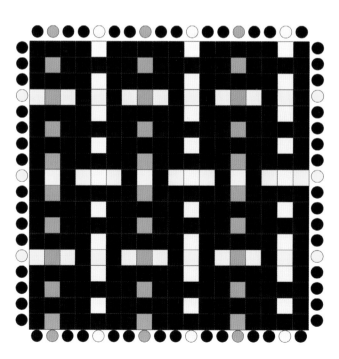

Dark Navy, Silver, White, Daffodil

Gradients

Plum, Purple, Green, Lime, Peacock, Turquoise, Blue, Black, White

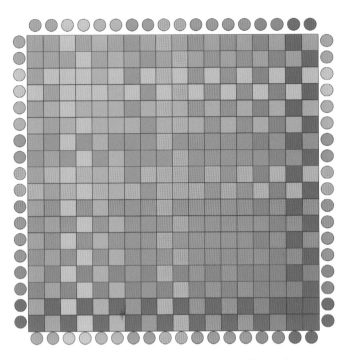

Robin's Egg, Powder Blue, Hydrangea, Lavender, Carnation, Salmon, Tiger Lily, Leaf, Peacock

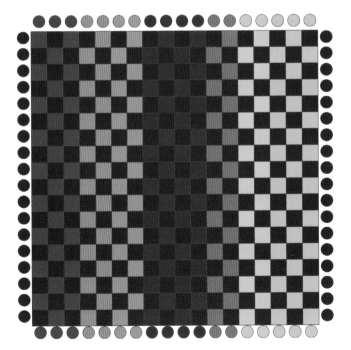

Plum, Pink, Salmon, Red, Orange, Yellow, Lime, Black

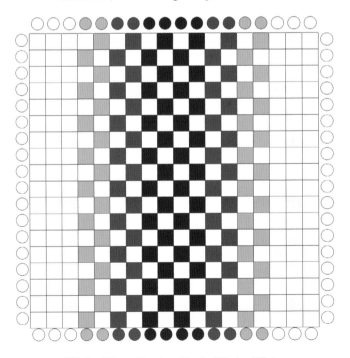

White, Silver, Pewter, Black, Winter White

Find the weaving pattern for this potholder on page 36.

Seasons: Fall

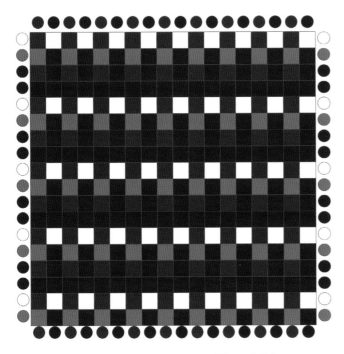

Spice, Burgundy, Chocolate, Winter White

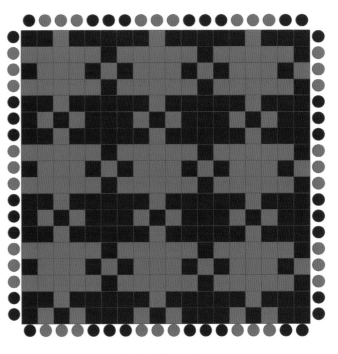

Spice, Chocolate

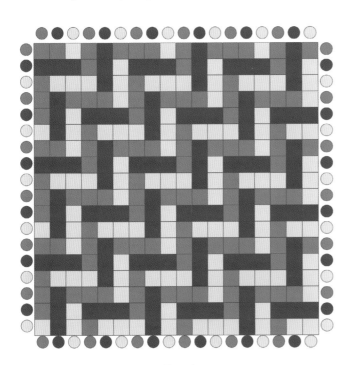

Willow, Flax, Autumn

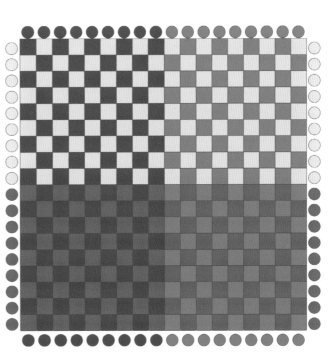

Willow, Flax, Autumn, Ochre

Seasons: Winter

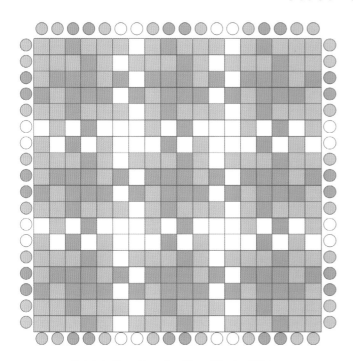

Robin's Egg, Powder Blue, Winter White

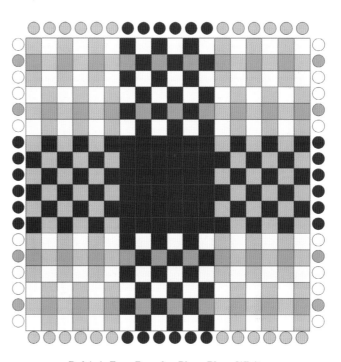

Robin's Egg, Powder Blue, Blue, White

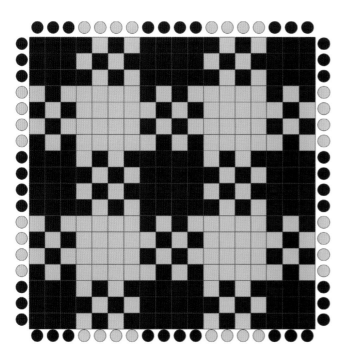

Dark Navy, Powder Blue

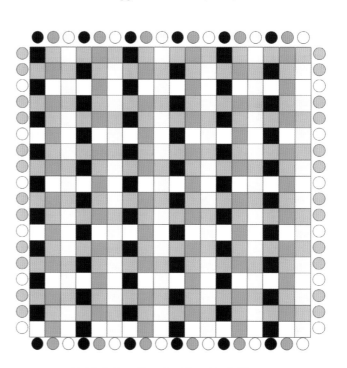

Robin's Egg, Powder Blue, Dark Navy,
White, Winter White

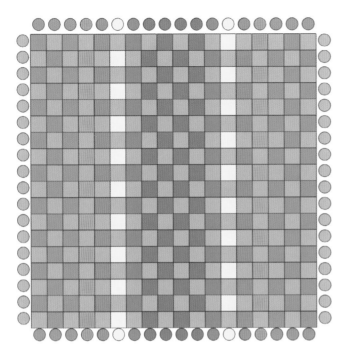

Robin's Egg, Powder Blue, Carnation, Tiger Lily,
Daffodil, Lavender, Leaf

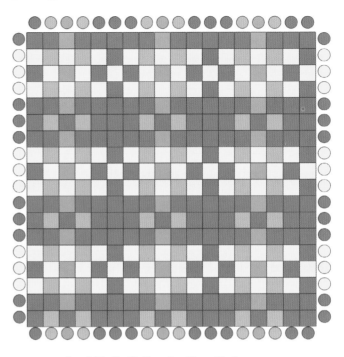

Leaf, Daffodil, Powder Blue, Hydrangea

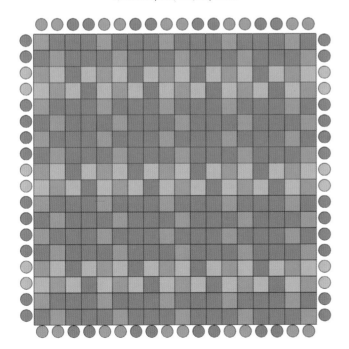

Leaf, Robin's Egg, Powder Blue

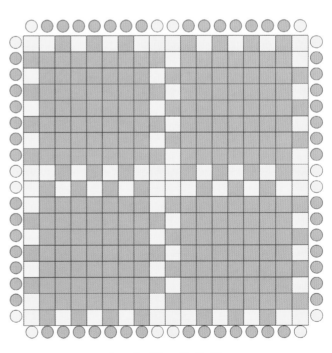

Powder Blue, Daffodil

Seasons: Summer

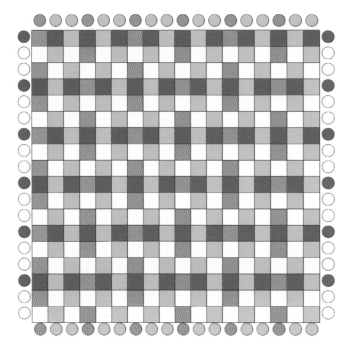

Peacock, Pink, Lime, White

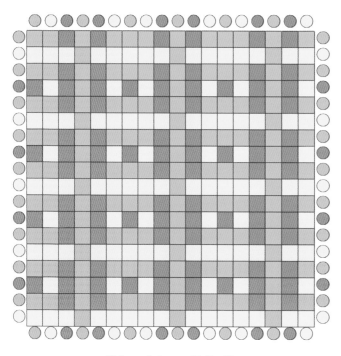

Yellow, Salmon, Daffodil

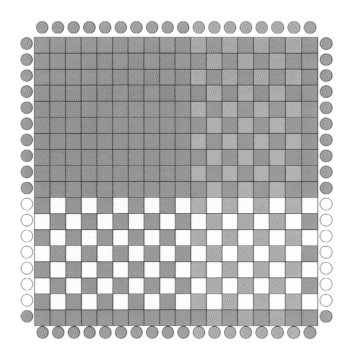

Salmon, Robin's Egg, Carnation, White

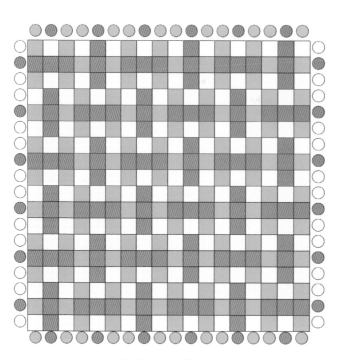

Pink, Lime, White

Abstract

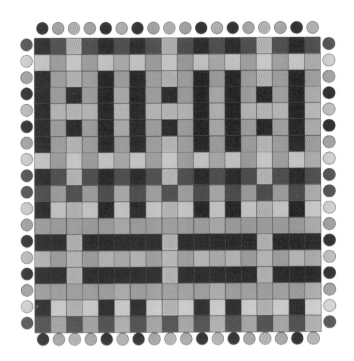

Purple, Hydrangea, Lavender, Carnation, Plum,
Powder Blue, Robin's Egg, Salmon

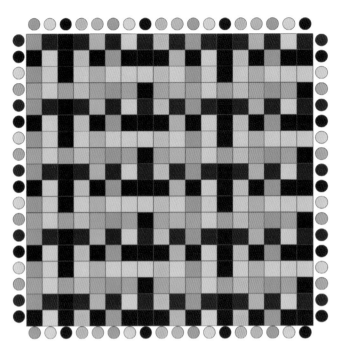

Leaf, Robin's Egg, Powder Blue, Burgundy,
Dark Navy, Salmon, Carnation

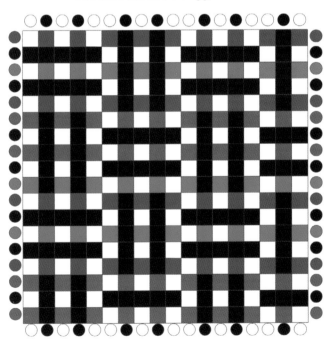

Winter White, Dark Navy, Autumn, Ochre, Pewter

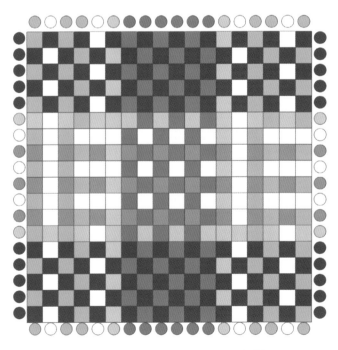

Willow, Winter White, Silver, Peacock, Lime,
Powder Blue, White

PRO Size Potholder Designs
& Supplies You'll Need

In this section you'll find designs for the PRO Potholder Loom. The sturdy metal PRO Potholder Loom measures 10" × 10" and makes 8" × 8" potholders.

All 34 loop colors are available both in Traditional and PRO size, inspiring endless design possibilities between the two looms.

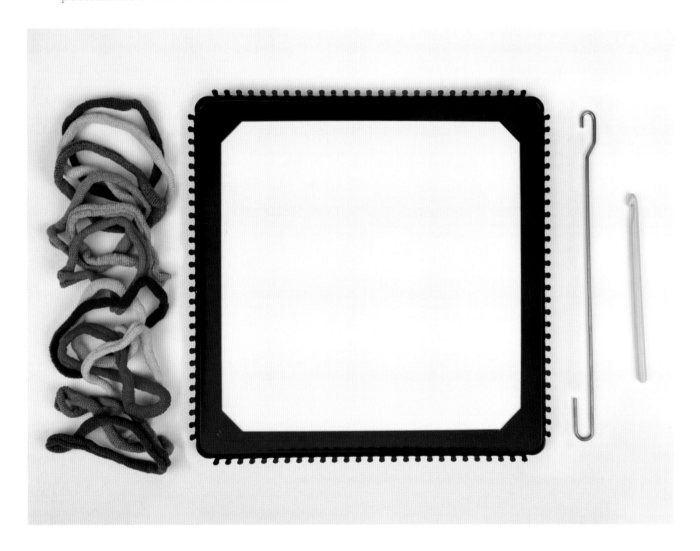

Bright Color Line

Find the weaving pattern for this potholder on page 46.

Plum, Purple, Pink, Salmon, Red, Orange, Yellow, Green,
Lime, Peacock, Turquoise, Blue, White

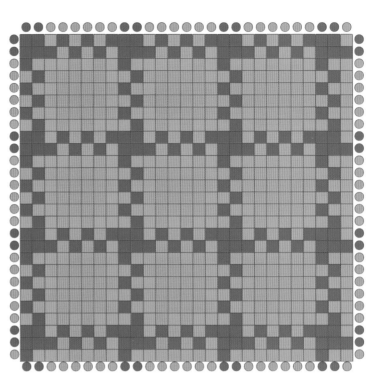

Salmon, Pink, Plum

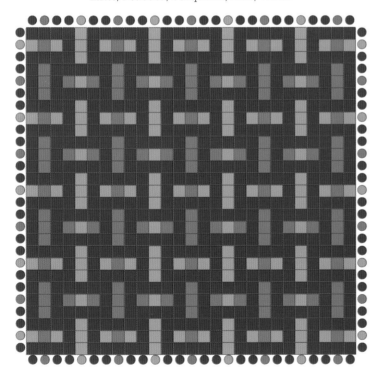

Blue, Turquoise, Peacock

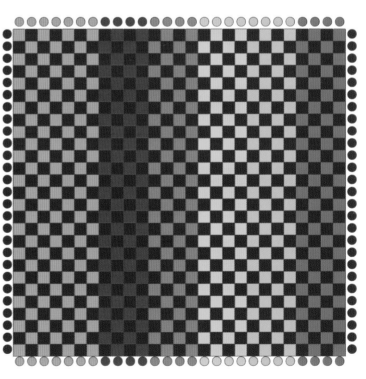

Pink, Salmon, Red, Orange, Yellow, Lime, Peacock, Black

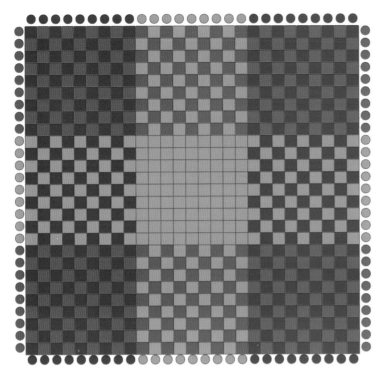

Plum, Purple, Turquoise

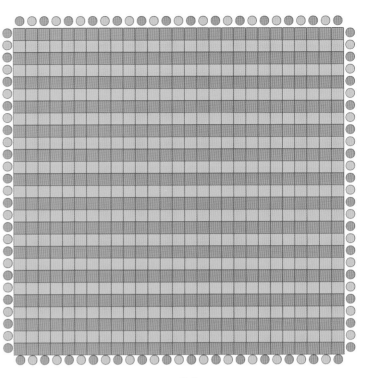

Pink, Yellow

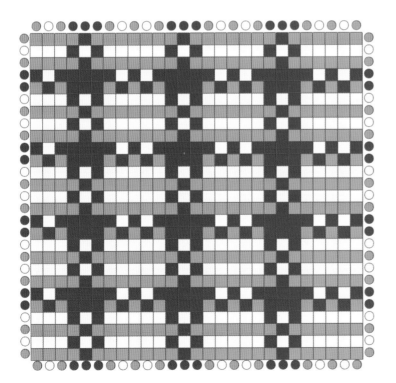

Salmon, Red, White

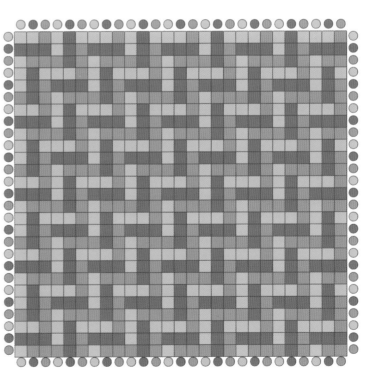

Lime, Peacock, Turquoise

Pastel Color Line

Find the weaving pattern for this potholder on page 49.

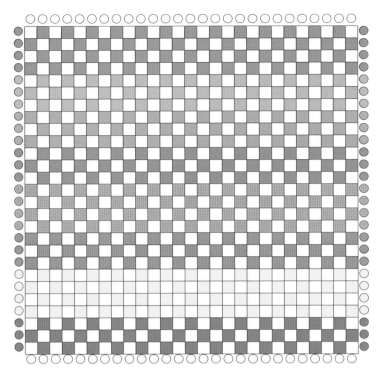

Robin's Egg, Powder Blue, Hydrangea, Lavender,
Carnation, Tiger Lily, Daffodil, Leaf, Winter White

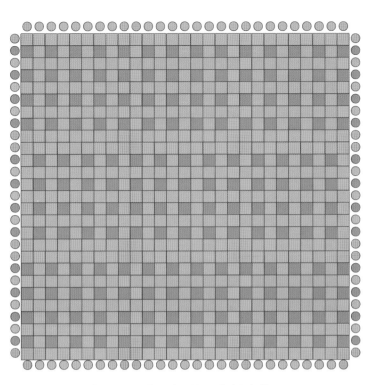

Carnation, Powder Blue, Robin's Egg

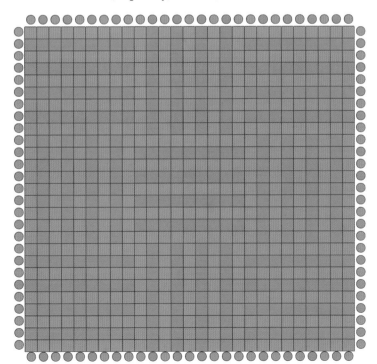

Robin's Egg, Lavender

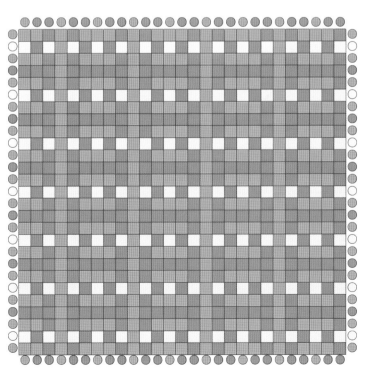

Carnation, Tiger Lily, White

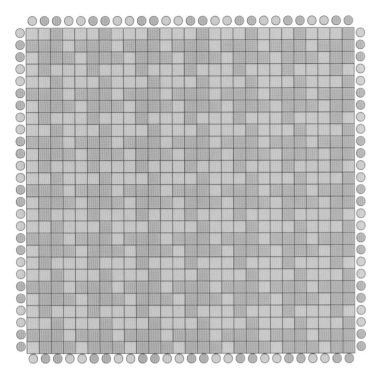

Powder Blue, Carnation

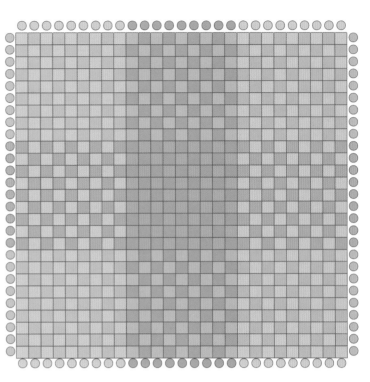

Robin's Egg, Powder Blue, Hydrangea, Lavender

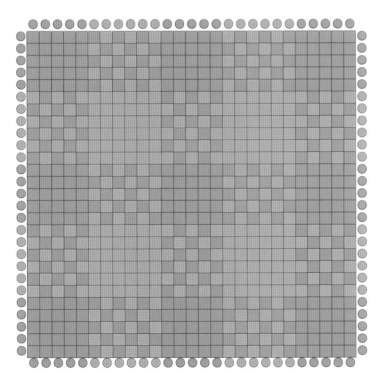

Carnation, Tiger Lily

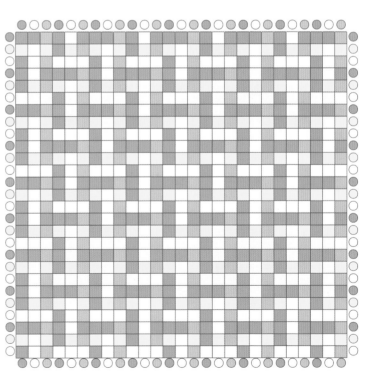

Robin's Egg, Powder Blue, Daffodil, White

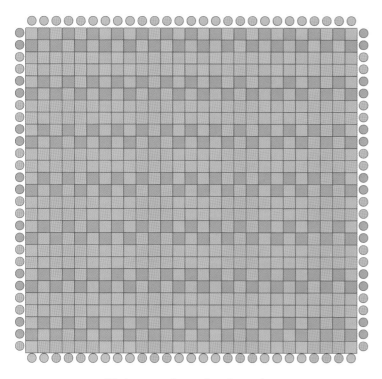

Hydrangea, Lavender, Carnation

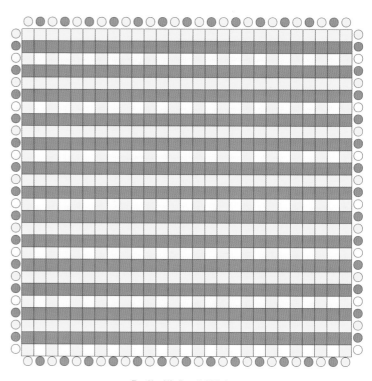

Daffodil, Leaf, White

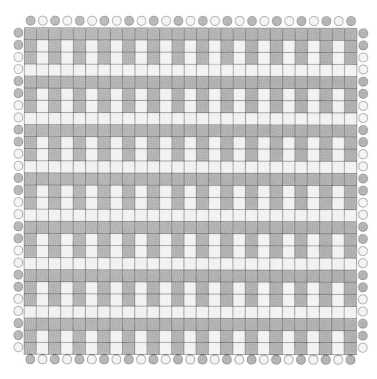

Carnation, Daffodil

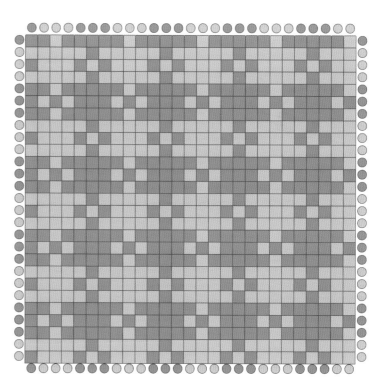

Powder Blue, Leaf

Designer Color Line

Find the weaving pattern for this potholder on page 53.

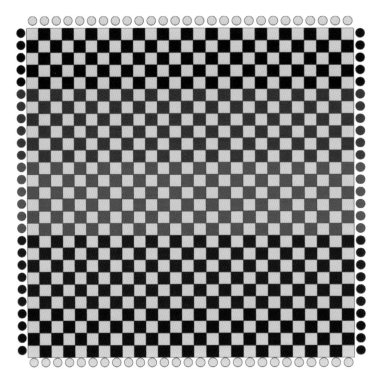

Pine, Willow, Ochre, Burgundy, Chocolate, Flax

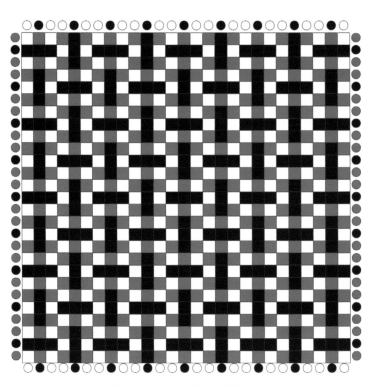

Pine, Autumn, Winter White

Winter White, Flax, Ochre, Spice, Autumn, Pine, Willow

Flax, Winter White

Flax, Willow, Autumn, Ochre

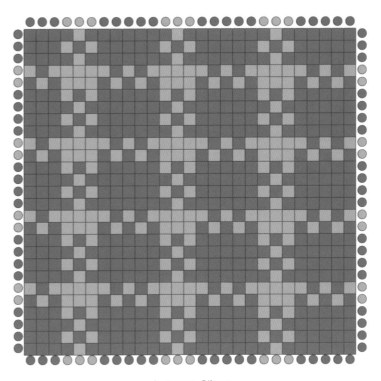

Autumn, Silver

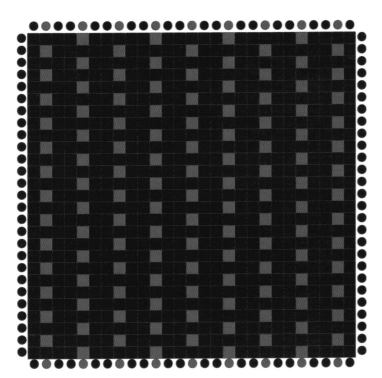

Burgundy, Spice

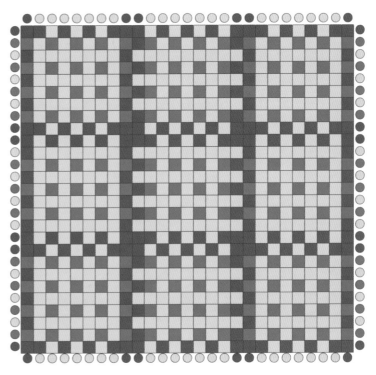

Ochre, Autumn, Flax

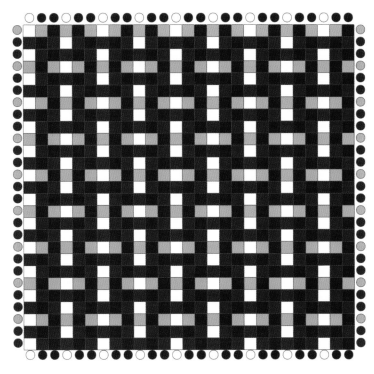

Burgundy, Chocolate, Silver, Winter White

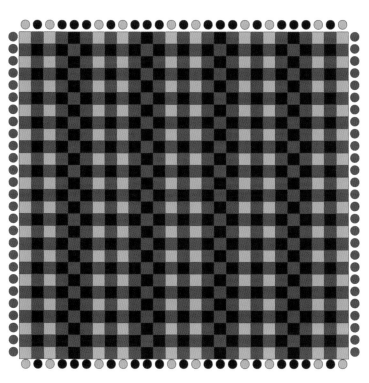

Silver, Pewter, Dark Navy

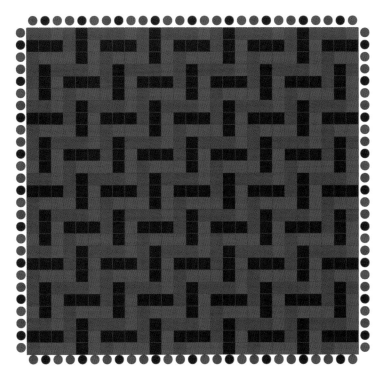

Willow, Pine, Pewter

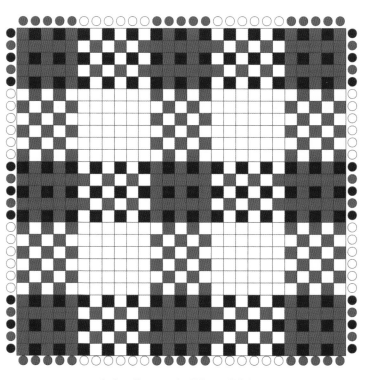

Spice, Burgundy, Winter White

Black & White

Black, White

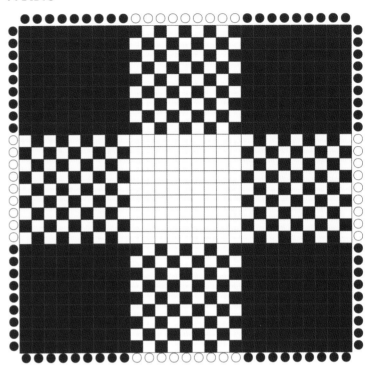

Black, White

Black, White

Black, White

One-Color

Lime, White

Peacock, White

Plum, White

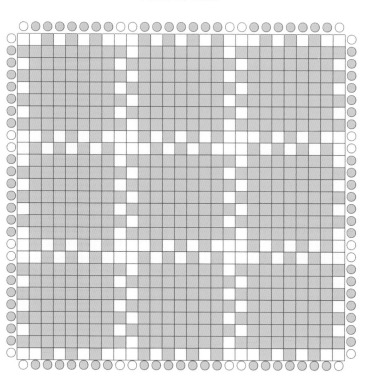

Yellow, White

Gradients

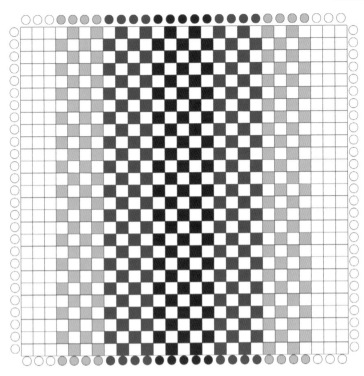

White, Silver, Pewter, Black, Winter White

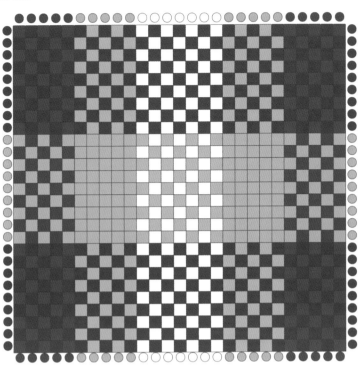

Willow, Pewter, Silver, Winter White

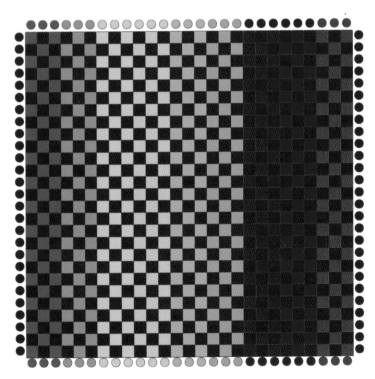

Green, Leaf, Lime, Powder Blue, Robin's Egg, Turquoise,
Blue, Purple, Plum, Black

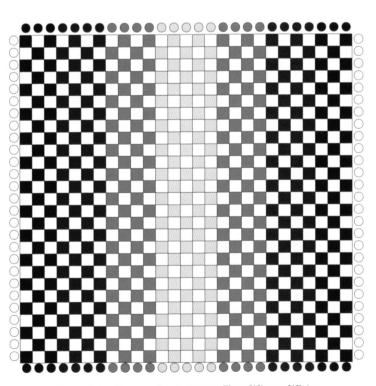

Chocolate, Burgundy, Autumn, Flax, Winter White

Multicolor

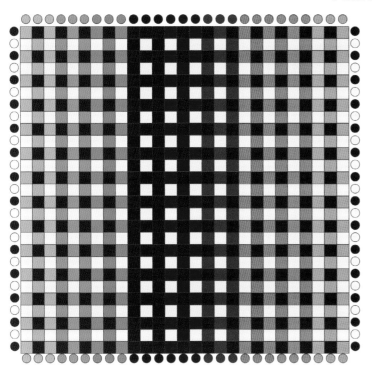

Powder Blue, Robin's Egg, Turquoise, Blue, Purple, Plum,
Pink, Salmon, Carnation, White, Black

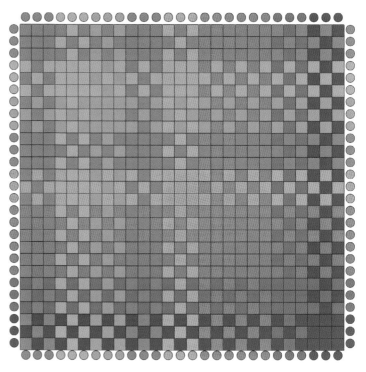

Robin's Egg, Powder Blue, Hydrangea, Lavender,
Carnation, Salmon, Tiger Lily, Leaf, Peacock

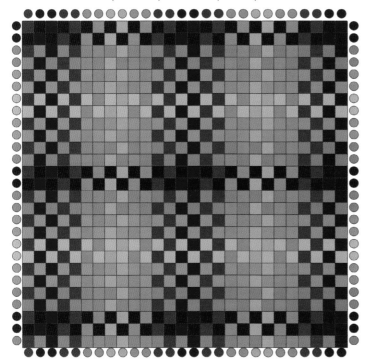

Blue, Plum, Purple, Robin's Egg, Powder Blue,
Hydrangea, Lavender

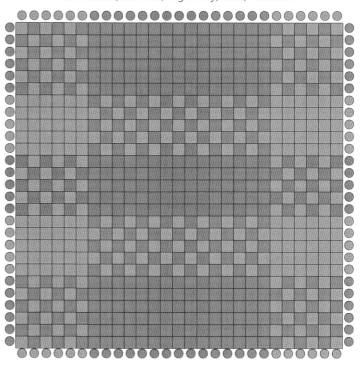

Carnation, Salmon, Pink

Abstract

Dark Navy, Willow, Silver, Powder Blue, Peacock, Leaf

Burgundy, Chocolate, Silver, Dark Navy, Flax, Autumn, Winter White, Pewter

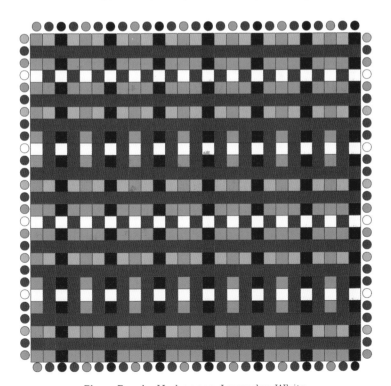

Plum, Purple, Hydrangea, Lavender, White

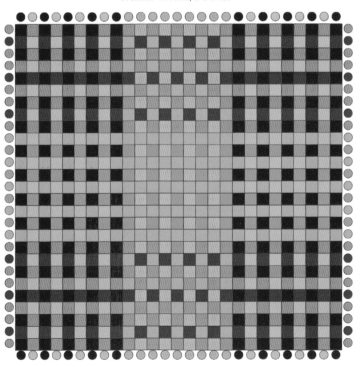

Plum, Purple, Robin's Egg, Powder Blue, Salmon, Carnation

Find the weaving pattern for this potholder on page 60.

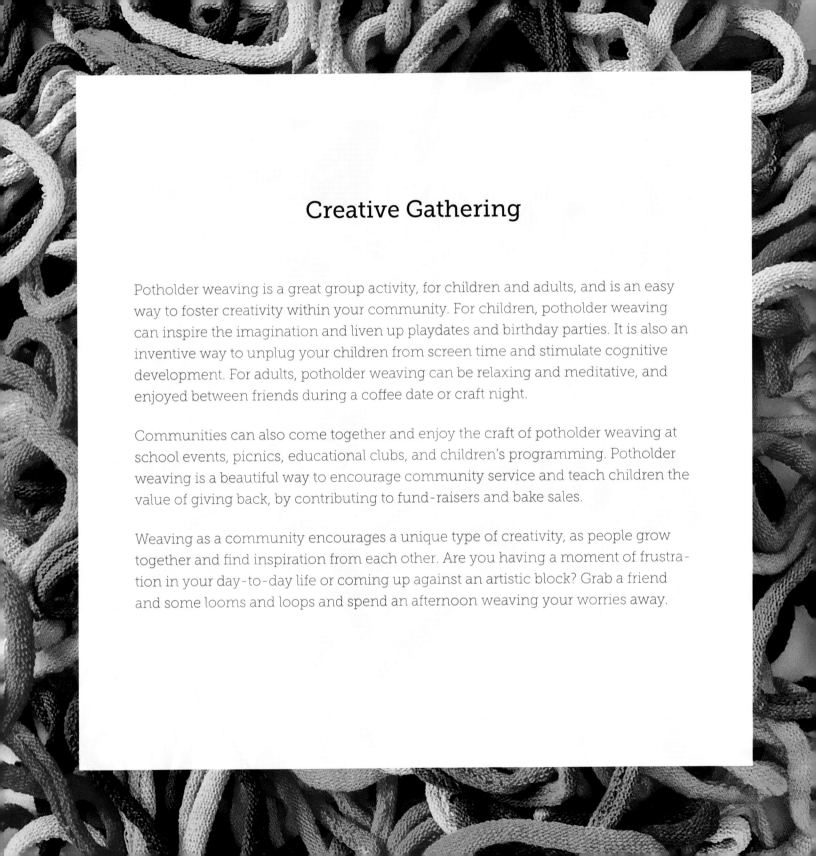

Creative Gathering

Potholder weaving is a great group activity, for children and adults, and is an easy way to foster creativity within your community. For children, potholder weaving can inspire the imagination and liven up playdates and birthday parties. It is also an inventive way to unplug your children from screen time and stimulate cognitive development. For adults, potholder weaving can be relaxing and meditative, and enjoyed between friends during a coffee date or craft night.

Communities can also come together and enjoy the craft of potholder weaving at school events, picnics, educational clubs, and children's programming. Potholder weaving is a beautiful way to encourage community service and teach children the value of giving back, by contributing to fund-raisers and bake sales.

Weaving as a community encourages a unique type of creativity, as people grow together and find inspiration from each other. Are you having a moment of frustration in your day-to-day life or coming up against an artistic block? Grab a friend and some looms and loops and spend an afternoon weaving your worries away.

Designed by Rachel Snack
Cover design by Danielle D. Farmer
Production design by Danielle D. Farmer
Type set in Museo Slab/MrsEavesItalic

ISBN: 978-0-7643-5850-0
Printed in China

All products shown are from the Friendly Loom™ by Harrisville Designs product line. This book was written and designed by weaver and artist Rachel Snack. Rachel is the founder of Weaver House Co., a textile studio dedicated to preserving craft tradition through handmaking and weaving education.

Published by Schiffer Publishing, Ltd.
4880 Lower Valley Road
Atglen, PA 19310
Phone: (610) 593-1777; Fax: (610) 593-2002
E-mail: Info@schifferbooks.com
Web: www.schifferbooks.com

For our complete selection of fine books on this and related subjects, please visit our website at www.schifferbooks.com. You may also write for a free catalog.

Schiffer Publishing's titles are available at special discounts for bulk purchases for sales promotions or premiums. Special editions, including personalized covers, corporate imprints, and excerpts, can be created in large quantities for special needs. For more information, contact the publisher.

We are always looking for people to write books on new and related subjects. If you have an idea for a book, please contact us at proposals@schifferbooks.com.

Other
SCHIFFER BOOKS
on Related Subjects:

  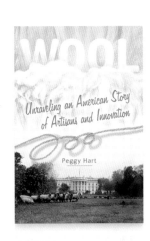

Welcome to Weaving: The Modern Guide,
Lindsey Campbell
ISBN 978-0-7643-5631-5

Threads Around the World: From Arabian Weaving to Batik in Zimbabwe,
Deb Brandon
ISBN 978-0-7643-5650-6

Wool: Unraveling an American Story of Artisans and Innovation,
Peggy Hart
ISBN 978-0-7643-5431-1